Caleb's Gumball Machine

By Caleb and Daddy

Original Copyright ©2015
ISBN 978-1-48358-979-4 ©2016

When Caleb was little, he was always asking his Mommy and Daddy to buy him stuff. Caleb's daddy usually said "No."

After a while, Caleb's daddy got tired of saying "No."
So he told Caleb to spend his own money.

Caleb didn't have any money.

Caleb asked a question, "Daddy, how do I get money?"

Daddy said, "Caleb, you get money by having ASSETS!"
"Oh," said Caleb.

Caleb scratched his head and looked puzzled.

Caleb asked, "What is an ASSET?"

"An ASSET is something that gets you money," said Daddy.

"Oh," said Caleb. "Like what?"

"Like a stock that pays a dividend," said Daddy.

"Huh?" said Caleb.

"Like a rental property," said Daddy.

"A what?" said Caleb.

"Like a Gumball Machine!" said Daddy.

"I know what a Gumball Machine is!" said Caleb.

They went to the Credit Union and Caleb got a 'loan' for $40 dollars.

They took the $40 and bought a Gumball Machine.

Then they went and bought a giant box of 800 gumballs.

Then Daddy asked a few places if Caleb could put the Gumball Machine there. Finally, a restaurant said yes. So, daddy helped Caleb put the Gumball Machine in the restaurant.

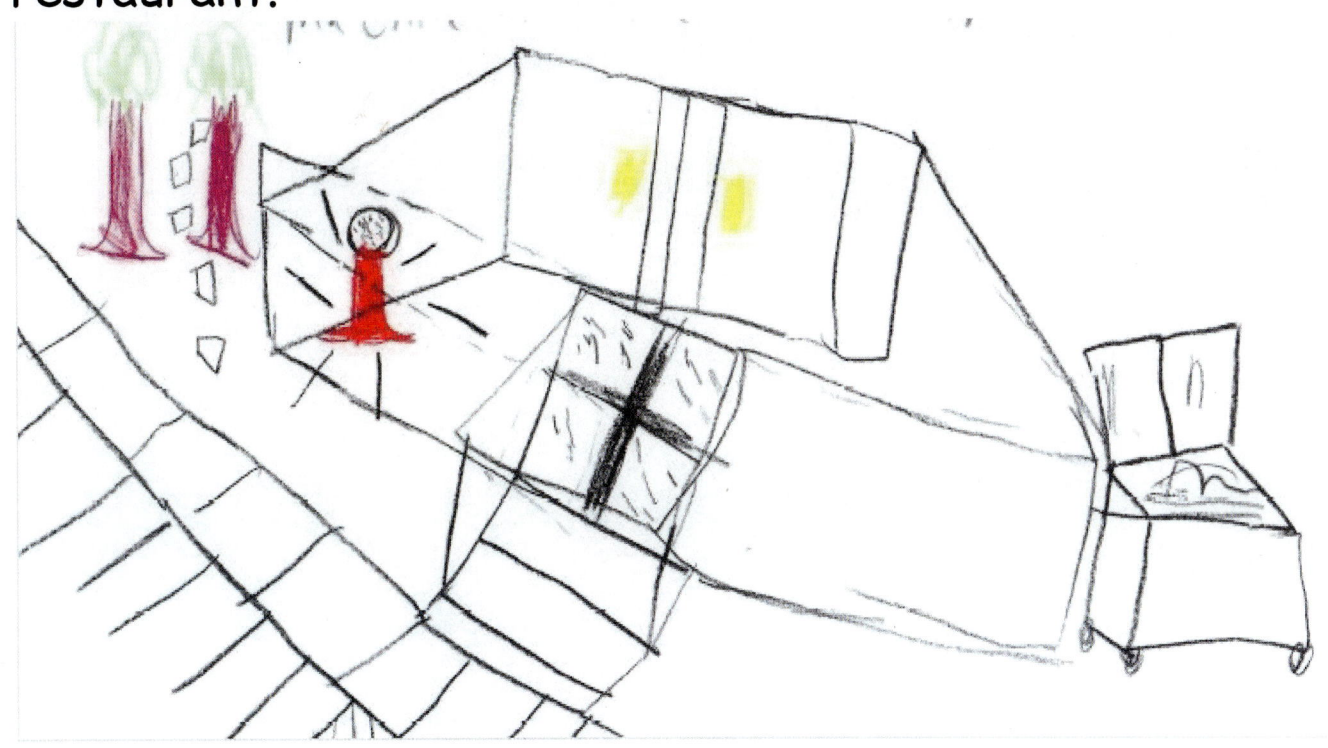

Then Caleb filled the Gumball Machine with gumballs.

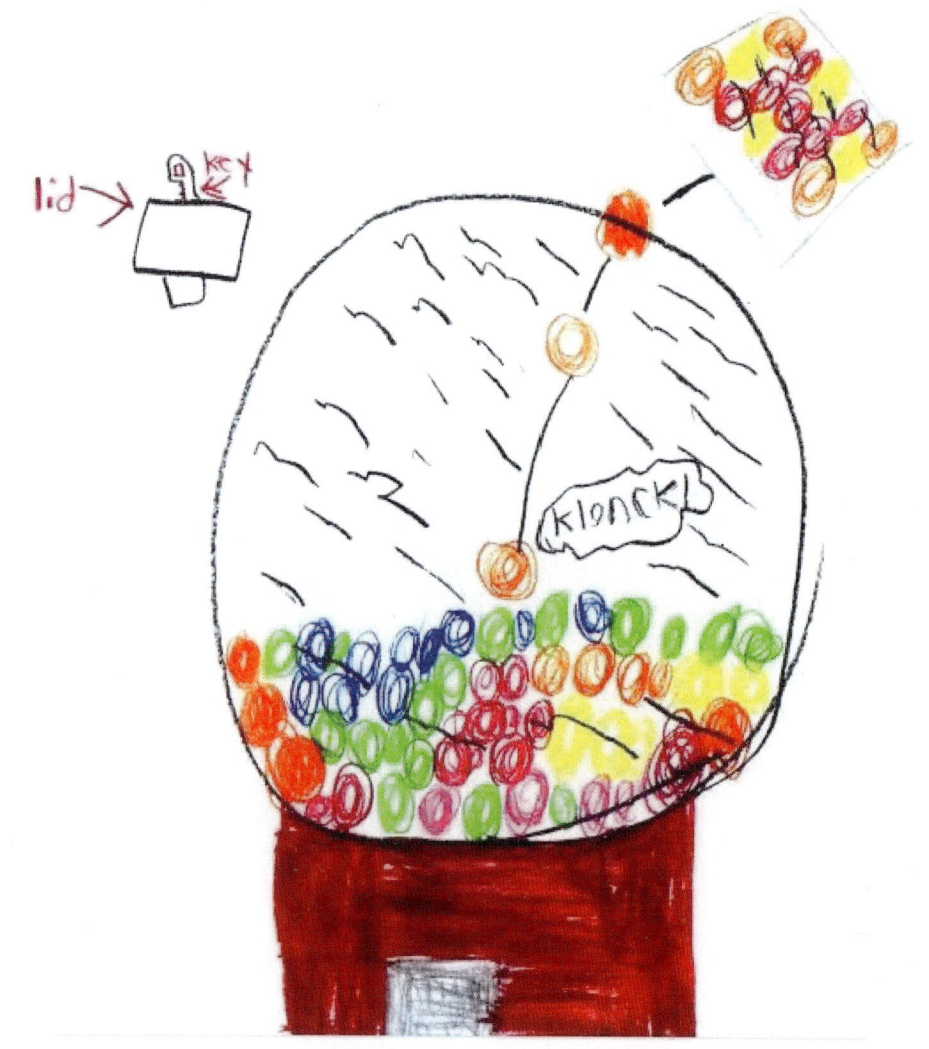

Then they left.

Caleb was not sure why they left the Gumball Machine at the restaurant!

One month later, Caleb and Daddy went back to the restaurant to check on the Gumball Machine. Some gumballs were gone.
"Where did they go?" asked Caleb.

Daddy opened the gumball machine for Caleb. It was full of quarters! "People bought gumballs from your Gumball Machine Caleb. Now you have an ASSET that gets you money. All of those quarters are yours!" said Daddy proudly.

Caleb got very excited.
"I'm rich!" said Caleb.
Caleb collected the coins.

The next month, they went back to the restaurant. Caleb's gumball machine was full of quarters again! This time, Caleb put in more gumballs then harvested the coins. Caleb was starting to get a lot of money.

After a few months, Caleb had paid back his loan and collected enough money to buy his own video games. He was very proud of himself.

Then, Daddy taught Caleb how to be smart with his money. They got 3 piggy banks. One piggy bank was for SAVINGS, one piggy bank was for INVESTING, and one piggy bank was for CHARITY.

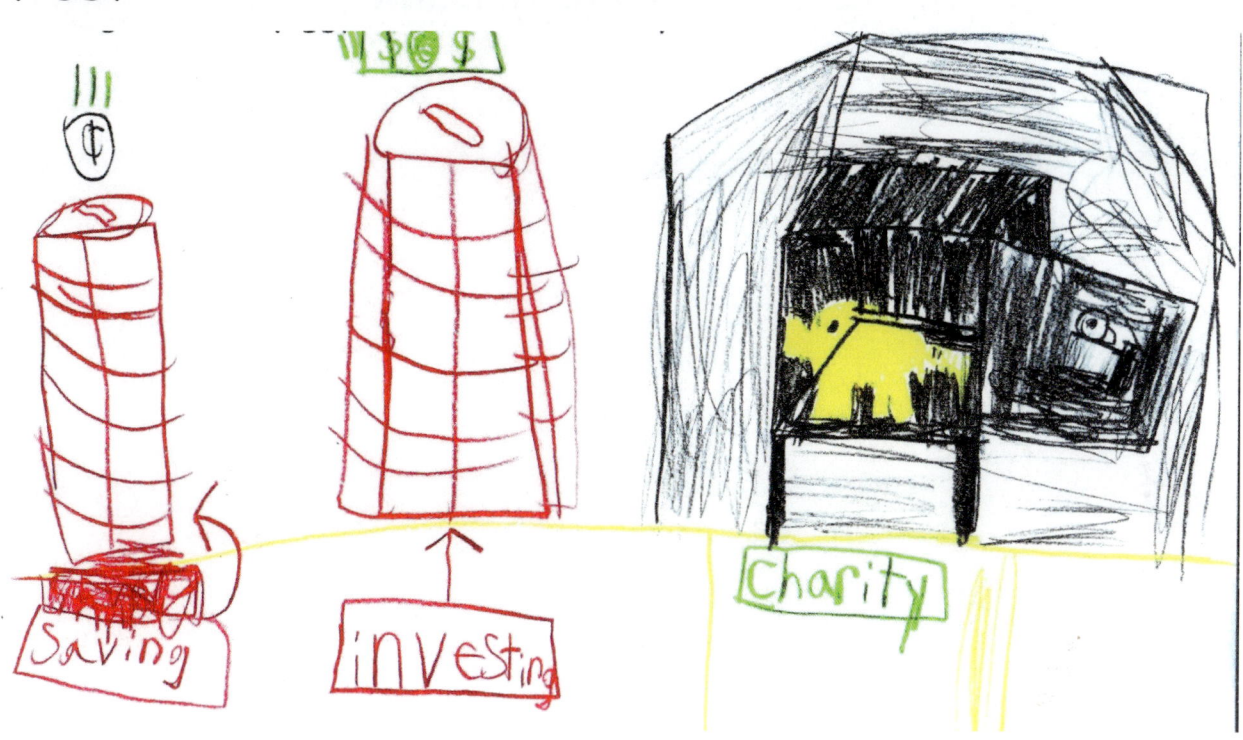

Now when Caleb gets money, he divides it up this way:

10% into his SAVINGS Piggy Bank
10% into his INVESTING Piggy Bank
10% into his CHARITY Piggy Bank

Caleb still has 70% left to spend on whatever he wants!

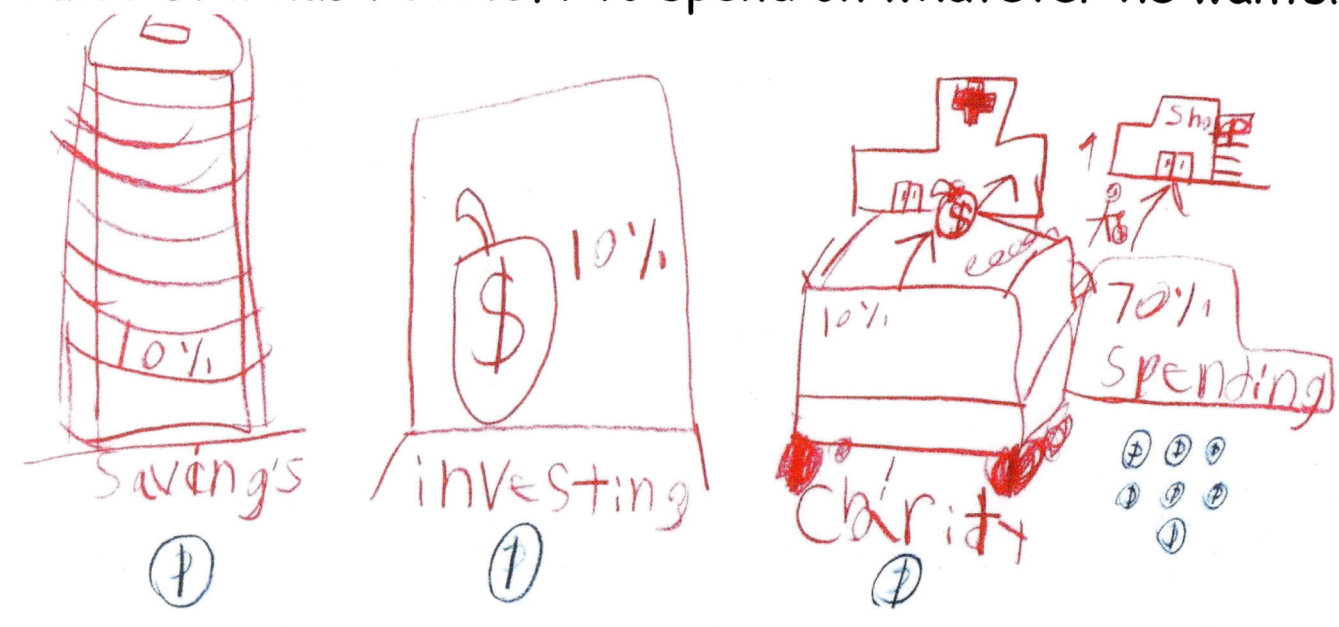

"Why do I need SAVINGS, Daddy?" asked Caleb. "Why can't I just spend all the money I get from my ASSET?"

"It is important to have SAVINGS so you can take care of unexpected problems," explained Daddy. "If your gumball machine breaks, you may need money to fix it, or buy a new one," said Daddy.

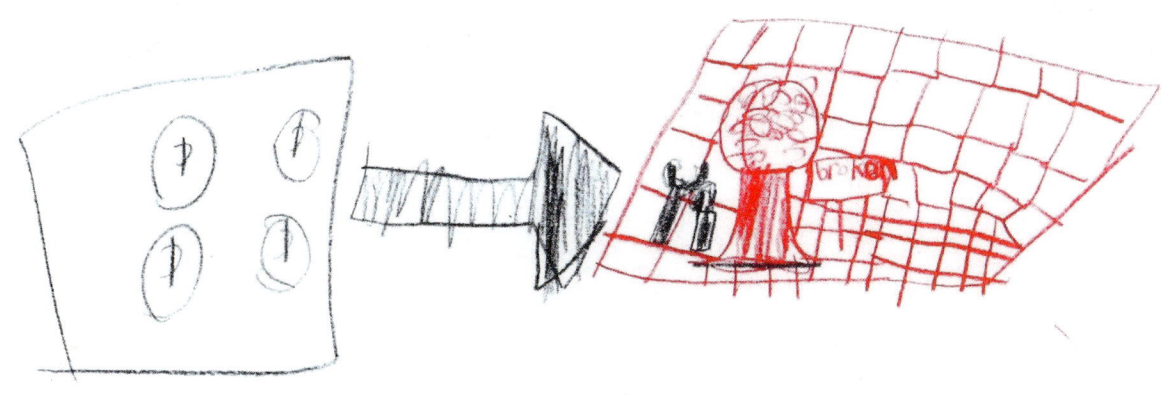

"Why do I need an INVESTING piggy bank then?" asked Caleb.

"You need an INVESTING piggy bank so that you can get more ASSETS," said Daddy. "Then instead of you working for money, you make your money work for you."

Caleb was excited to learn that he could have more than one ASSET!

Caleb's favorite account is his CHARITY Piggy Bank.
He gives 10% to his Church or a CHARITY.
His favorite CHARITY helps sick kids feel better.

After a few months of collecting coins from the gumball machine, each account began to have a lot of money. Caleb now has lots of money in SAVINGS, lots of money for INVESTING, and lots of money to give to CHARITY.

He also has lots to spend!
Now Caleb buys whatever he wants with his own money.

"Do you like having ASSETS?!" said Daddy.

"I sure Do!" said Caleb.

The End

Caleb reading a book from Daddy's bookshelf: "Retire Young, Retire Rich", by Robert Kiyosaki and Sharon Lechter.

Caleb gets a 'loan' for $40.

Caleb buys a new Gumball Machine for $40.

Daddy buys a box of gumballs.

Caleb collects coins from inside the gumball machine.

Caleb starts to get a lot of money.

Caleb adds more gumballs to the Gumball Machine.

Caleb buys himself a video game system and video games.

Now Caleb buys himself whatever he wants with his own money.
Do you want an ASSET too? :-)

Join us on Facebook to interact with Caleb and Daddy and other fans of 'Caleb's Gumball Machine'
http://www.facebook.com/CalebsGumballMachine/

Subscribe to our YouTube channel called 'Caleb's Gumball Machine' at:
https://www.youtube.com/channel/UCTAyMWYvoCyMYWz2dJHBBEw

Teachers – To create, purchase or share curriculum for your class using this book visit:
http://www.TeachersPayTeachers.com
Please kindly include our website address (below) on each page of materials you create.

A very special THANK-YOU to Our 'Backers' on Kickstarter for making this book come to life!

Visit our Official Site on the Web at:
http://www.CalebsGumballMachine.com